50 Vegan Cheese Making Recipes for Home

By: Kelly Johnson

Table of Contents

- Cashew Mozzarella
- Almond Feta
- Vegan Cream Cheese
- Nut-Free Cheese Sauce
- Tofu Ricotta
- Smoked Paprika Cashew Cheese
- Herbed Cashew Spread
- Garlic and Dill Hemp Seed Cheese
- Sunflower Seed Cheddar
- Basil and Lemon Macadamia Cheese
- Vegan Brie
- Vegan Gouda
- Spicy Sriracha Cheese
- Walnut and Cranberry Cheese Ball
- Vegan Parmesan
- Vegan Queso Dip
- Pine Nut Cheese Spread
- Truffle Almond Cheese
- Pesto Cashew Cheese
- Chipotle Cashew Cheese
- Vegan Nacho Cheese Sauce
- Sun-Dried Tomato and Basil Cashew Cheese
- Roasted Red Pepper and Walnut Spread
- Vegan Blue Cheese
- Hemp and Chive Cream Cheese
- Cashew and Sundried Tomato Spread
- Vegan Havarti
- Vegan Swiss Cheese
- Pistachio and Cranberry Cheese Log
- Za'atar-Spiced Almond Cheese
- Vegan Beer Cheese
- Vegan Miso Butter
- Turmeric and Black Pepper Cashew Cheese
- Raspberry and Walnut Cream Cheese
- Caramelized Onion and Thyme Almond Cheese

- Vegan Quesadilla Cheese
- Vegan Greek-style Feta
- Vegan White Chocolate Cream Cheese
- Pecan and Cranberry Cheese Ball
- Vegan Ricotta Stuffed Shells
- Vegan Pimento Cheese
- Cumin and Coriander Seed Cheese
- Vegan Tzatziki
- Walnut and Herb Stuffed Mushrooms
- Vegan Cheesecake with Berry Compote
- Cashew and Chive Cheese Ball
- Vegan Pepper Jack Cheese
- Vegan Tandoori Cheese
- Vegan Garlic and Herb Boursin
- Vegan Cheesy Kale Chips

Cashew Mozzarella

Ingredients:

- 1 cup raw cashews, soaked in water for at least 4 hours or overnight
- 1/4 cup nutritional yeast
- 2 tablespoons tapioca starch
- 1 tablespoon lemon juice
- 1 teaspoon apple cider vinegar
- 1/2 teaspoon garlic powder
- 1/2 teaspoon onion powder
- 1/2 teaspoon salt
- 1 1/2 cups water

Instructions:

Soak Cashews:
- Place the raw cashews in a bowl and cover them with water. Allow them to soak for at least 4 hours or overnight. Drain and rinse before using.

Blend Cashews:
- In a blender, combine the soaked cashews, nutritional yeast, tapioca starch, lemon juice, apple cider vinegar, garlic powder, onion powder, salt, and water. Blend until smooth and creamy.

Cook Mixture:
- Transfer the blended mixture to a saucepan over medium heat. Stir continuously as the mixture thickens. It will start to clump together and become stretchy.

Continue Cooking:
- Keep stirring until the mixture forms a thick, gooey consistency. This usually takes about 5-7 minutes.

Cooling:
- Once the cashew mixture has thickened, remove it from the heat and let it cool for a few minutes. It will become stretchier as it cools.

Shape or Store:
- At this point, you can shape the cashew mozzarella into balls or use it as a spreadable cheese. If you want it to be more solid, transfer it to a container and refrigerate until set.

Usage:

- Use cashew mozzarella in various dishes like pizza, lasagna, sandwiches, or salads. It melts well and adds a creamy texture to your favorite recipes.

Enjoy your homemade cashew mozzarella as a tasty and cruelty-free alternative to traditional dairy-based mozzarella. Feel free to adjust the seasonings to suit your taste preferences.

Almond Feta

Ingredients:

- 1 cup blanched almonds, soaked in water for at least 4 hours or overnight
- 3 tablespoons lemon juice
- 2 tablespoons apple cider vinegar
- 1/4 cup nutritional yeast
- 2 cloves garlic, minced
- 1/2 teaspoon salt
- 1/4 cup extra virgin olive oil
- Water (as needed for blending)
- Fresh herbs (optional, for garnish)

Instructions:

Soak Almonds:
- Place the blanched almonds in a bowl and cover them with water. Allow them to soak for at least 4 hours or overnight. Drain and rinse before using.

Blend Ingredients:
- In a blender or food processor, combine the soaked almonds, lemon juice, apple cider vinegar, nutritional yeast, minced garlic, and salt. Blend until you achieve a smooth and creamy consistency.

Adjust Consistency:
- If the mixture is too thick, you can add a little water, one tablespoon at a time, until you reach your desired consistency.

Shape the Feta:
- Transfer the almond mixture to a piece of cheesecloth or a clean kitchen towel. Twist and squeeze to remove excess moisture.

Set in the Refrigerator:
- Place the shaped almond mixture on a plate or in a container and refrigerate for at least 2-4 hours to allow it to firm up.

Finish with Olive Oil:
- Once set, drizzle extra virgin olive oil over the almond feta for added flavor. Optionally, sprinkle fresh herbs on top for garnish.

Serve:
- Use almond feta in salads, on crackers, in sandwiches, or any dish where you would use traditional feta cheese.

Enjoy your homemade almond feta! This dairy-free alternative is rich in flavor and can be a great addition to your plant-based culinary repertoire.

Vegan Cream Cheese

Ingredients:

- 1 cup raw cashews, soaked in water for at least 4 hours or overnight
- 2 tablespoons nutritional yeast
- 2 tablespoons lemon juice
- 1 tablespoon apple cider vinegar
- 1 clove garlic, minced
- 1/2 teaspoon salt
- 2 tablespoons refined coconut oil, melted (optional, for a creamier texture)
- Water (as needed for blending)

Instructions:

Soak Cashews:
- Place the raw cashews in a bowl and cover them with water. Allow them to soak for at least 4 hours or overnight. Drain and rinse before using.

Blend Ingredients:
- In a blender or food processor, combine the soaked cashews, nutritional yeast, lemon juice, apple cider vinegar, minced garlic, and salt.

Blend Until Smooth:
- Blend until the mixture becomes smooth and creamy. If it's too thick, you can add water, one tablespoon at a time, until you reach your desired consistency.

Add Coconut Oil (Optional):
- For a creamier texture, you can add melted refined coconut oil to the mixture and blend again until well combined.

Adjust Seasoning:
- Taste the cream cheese and adjust the seasonings as needed. You can add more lemon juice, salt, or nutritional yeast to suit your preferences.

Chill:
- Transfer the vegan cream cheese to a container and refrigerate for at least 2 hours to allow it to firm up.

Serve:
- Use the vegan cream cheese as a spread on bagels, toast, crackers, or in your favorite recipes.

Feel free to experiment with additional flavors by incorporating herbs, garlic, chives, or other seasonings to suit your taste. This vegan cream cheese is a versatile and delicious dairy-free alternative.

Nut-Free Cheese Sauce

Ingredients:

- 1 cup peeled and diced potatoes
- 1/2 cup peeled and diced carrots
- 1/4 cup nutritional yeast
- 1/4 cup refined coconut oil or vegan butter
- 1/2 cup unsweetened plant-based milk (such as almond, soy, or oat milk)
- 1 tablespoon lemon juice
- 1 teaspoon onion powder
- 1 teaspoon garlic powder
- 1/2 teaspoon mustard (optional for flavor)
- Salt and pepper to taste
- Paprika for garnish (optional)

Instructions:

Boil Potatoes and Carrots:
- In a pot, boil the diced potatoes and carrots until they are fork-tender. This usually takes about 10-15 minutes.

Blend Ingredients:
- In a blender, combine the boiled potatoes, carrots, nutritional yeast, coconut oil or vegan butter, plant-based milk, lemon juice, onion powder, garlic powder, and optional mustard. Blend until smooth and creamy.

Adjust Consistency:
- If the sauce is too thick, you can add more plant-based milk, a tablespoon at a time, until you reach your desired consistency.

Season to Taste:
- Add salt and pepper to taste. You can also adjust the lemon juice, nutritional yeast, or other seasonings according to your preference.

Serve:
- Pour the nut-free cheese sauce over pasta, vegetables, or use it as a dip. You can also heat it gently on the stove if you prefer a warm sauce.

Garnish (Optional):
- Sprinkle with paprika or any other herbs of your choice for additional flavor and presentation.

This nut-free cheese sauce is a versatile and allergy-friendly alternative, perfect for various dishes where you'd use a traditional cheese sauce. Feel free to customize it to suit your taste preferences.

Tofu Ricotta

Ingredients:

- 1 block (about 14-16 ounces) extra-firm tofu, pressed and drained
- 2 tablespoons nutritional yeast
- 2 tablespoons lemon juice
- 2 tablespoons olive oil
- 2 cloves garlic, minced
- 1 teaspoon dried basil
- 1 teaspoon dried oregano
- 1/2 teaspoon salt (or to taste)
- 1/4 teaspoon black pepper
- Optional: Fresh herbs such as parsley or basil for garnish

Instructions:

Press and Drain Tofu:
- Press the tofu to remove excess water. You can do this by wrapping the block of tofu in a clean kitchen towel and placing something heavy on top (like a cast-iron skillet) for about 15-30 minutes. Once pressed, crumble the tofu into a bowl.

Prepare Tofu Mixture:
- Add nutritional yeast, lemon juice, olive oil, minced garlic, dried basil, dried oregano, salt, and black pepper to the crumbled tofu.

Mix Well:
- Mix all the ingredients thoroughly until well combined. You can use a fork or your hands to ensure the mixture is evenly mixed.

Taste and Adjust:
- Taste the tofu ricotta and adjust the seasonings according to your preferences. You might want to add more salt, nutritional yeast, or lemon juice for extra flavor.

Optional Blend:
- If you prefer a smoother consistency, you can transfer the mixture to a food processor and pulse until it reaches your desired texture.

Chill (Optional):
- You can use the tofu ricotta immediately, or for a firmer texture and enhanced flavors, refrigerate it for at least an hour.

Serve:
- Use tofu ricotta in dishes like lasagna, stuffed shells, or as a spread on toast or crackers. Garnish with fresh herbs if desired.

This tofu ricotta provides a creamy, dairy-free alternative with a texture and flavor reminiscent of traditional ricotta. Feel free to experiment with additional herbs and spices to suit your taste preferences.

Smoked Paprika Cashew Cheese

Ingredients:

- 1 cup raw cashews, soaked in water for at least 4 hours or overnight
- 2 tablespoons nutritional yeast
- 1 tablespoon lemon juice
- 2 tablespoons olive oil
- 1 clove garlic, minced
- 1 teaspoon smoked paprika
- 1/2 teaspoon salt (or to taste)
- Water (as needed for blending)

Instructions:

Soak Cashews:
- Place the raw cashews in a bowl and cover them with water. Allow them to soak for at least 4 hours or overnight. Drain and rinse before using.

Blend Ingredients:
- In a blender or food processor, combine the soaked cashews, nutritional yeast, lemon juice, olive oil, minced garlic, smoked paprika, and salt.

Blend Until Smooth:
- Blend the ingredients until you achieve a smooth and creamy consistency. If the mixture is too thick, add water, one tablespoon at a time, until you reach the desired texture.

Adjust Seasoning:
- Taste the cashew cheese and adjust the salt or smoked paprika to your liking.

Serve:
- Transfer the smoked paprika cashew cheese to a bowl and use it as a spread on crackers, bread, or as a dip for veggies.

Chill (Optional):
- For a firmer texture and to enhance the flavors, you can refrigerate the cashew cheese for at least an hour before serving.

Garnish (Optional):
- Garnish with a sprinkle of additional smoked paprika on top for extra flavor and presentation.

This smoked paprika cashew cheese is a delicious and versatile plant-based alternative, perfect for adding a smoky kick to your dishes or as a delightful appetizer. Enjoy experimenting with different herbs and spices to customize the flavor to your liking.

Herbed Cashew Spread

Ingredients:

- 1 cup raw cashews, soaked in water for at least 4 hours or overnight
- 2 tablespoons nutritional yeast
- 1 tablespoon lemon juice
- 2 tablespoons olive oil
- 1 clove garlic, minced
- 1 tablespoon fresh parsley, chopped
- 1 tablespoon fresh chives, chopped
- 1 teaspoon dried thyme
- Salt and pepper to taste
- Water (as needed for blending)

Instructions:

Soak Cashews:
- Place the raw cashews in a bowl and cover them with water. Allow them to soak for at least 4 hours or overnight. Drain and rinse before using.

Blend Ingredients:
- In a blender or food processor, combine the soaked cashews, nutritional yeast, lemon juice, olive oil, minced garlic, fresh parsley, fresh chives, dried thyme, salt, and pepper.

Blend Until Smooth:
- Blend the ingredients until you achieve a smooth and creamy consistency. If the mixture is too thick, add water, one tablespoon at a time, until you reach the desired texture.

Adjust Seasoning:
- Taste the herbed cashew spread and adjust the salt, pepper, or herbs to your liking.

Serve:
- Transfer the herbed cashew spread to a bowl and use it as a dip with vegetables, crackers, or bread. It can also be used as a spread in sandwiches or wraps.

Chill (Optional):
- For a firmer texture and to allow the flavors to meld, you can refrigerate the cashew spread for at least an hour before serving.

Garnish (Optional):
- Garnish with additional fresh herbs for extra flavor and presentation.

Feel free to experiment with different herbs like basil, dill, or cilantro to customize the spread to your taste preferences. This herbed cashew spread is a delightful addition to your plant-based repertoire.

Garlic and Dill Hemp Seed Cheese

Ingredients:

- 1 cup shelled hemp seeds
- 2 tablespoons nutritional yeast
- 2 tablespoons lemon juice
- 2 tablespoons olive oil
- 2 cloves garlic, minced
- 1 tablespoon fresh dill, chopped (or 1 teaspoon dried dill)
- 1/2 teaspoon onion powder
- Salt and pepper to taste
- Water (as needed for blending)

Instructions:

Blend Ingredients:
- In a blender or food processor, combine the hemp seeds, nutritional yeast, lemon juice, olive oil, minced garlic, fresh dill, onion powder, salt, and pepper.

Blend Until Smooth:
- Blend the ingredients until you achieve a smooth and creamy consistency. If the mixture is too thick, add water, one tablespoon at a time, until you reach the desired texture.

Adjust Seasoning:
- Taste the hemp seed cheese and adjust the salt, pepper, or herbs to your liking.

Serve:
- Transfer the garlic and dill hemp seed cheese to a bowl and use it as a dip with vegetables, crackers, or bread. It can also be used as a spread in sandwiches or wraps.

Chill (Optional):
- For a firmer texture and to allow the flavors to meld, you can refrigerate the hemp seed cheese for at least an hour before serving.

Garnish (Optional):
- Garnish with additional fresh dill for extra flavor and presentation.

This garlic and dill hemp seed cheese is a delightful and nutrient-rich alternative, providing a unique twist to your plant-based spreads. Enjoy experimenting with different herbs and spices to customize the flavor to your liking.

Sunflower Seed Cheddar

Ingredients:

- 1 cup raw sunflower seeds, soaked in water for at least 4 hours or overnight
- 2 tablespoons nutritional yeast
- 1 tablespoon lemon juice
- 1 tablespoon apple cider vinegar
- 2 cloves garlic, minced
- 1 teaspoon onion powder
- 1 teaspoon Dijon mustard
- 1/2 teaspoon turmeric powder (for color)
- 1/2 teaspoon smoked paprika
- Salt to taste
- Water (as needed for blending)

Instructions:

Soak Sunflower Seeds:
- Place the raw sunflower seeds in a bowl and cover them with water. Allow them to soak for at least 4 hours or overnight. Drain and rinse before using.

Blend Ingredients:
- In a blender or food processor, combine the soaked sunflower seeds, nutritional yeast, lemon juice, apple cider vinegar, minced garlic, onion powder, Dijon mustard, turmeric powder, smoked paprika, and salt.

Blend Until Smooth:
- Blend the ingredients until you achieve a smooth and creamy consistency. If the mixture is too thick, add water, one tablespoon at a time, until you reach the desired texture.

Adjust Seasoning:
- Taste the sunflower seed cheddar and adjust the salt, spices, or acidity to your liking.

Shape (Optional):
- If you want to mold the cheddar, transfer the mixture to a piece of cheesecloth or a clean kitchen towel. Twist and squeeze to remove excess moisture.

Chill (Optional):

- For a firmer texture, refrigerate the sunflower seed cheddar for at least 2-4 hours.

Serve:
- Use sunflower seed cheddar as a spread on crackers, bread, or in sandwiches. It's also great for melting in recipes like quesadillas or grilled cheese sandwiches.

Feel free to experiment with additional herbs and spices to customize the flavor of your sunflower seed cheddar. This recipe offers a delicious, nut-free cheese alternative that is perfect for various dishes.

Basil and Lemon Macadamia Cheese

Ingredients:

- 1 cup raw macadamia nuts, soaked in water for at least 4 hours or overnight
- 2 tablespoons nutritional yeast
- 2 tablespoons lemon juice
- 1 tablespoon apple cider vinegar
- 1 clove garlic, minced
- 1 cup fresh basil leaves, packed
- 1/4 cup extra virgin olive oil
- Salt and pepper to taste
- Water (as needed for blending)

Instructions:

Soak Macadamia Nuts:
- Place the raw macadamia nuts in a bowl and cover them with water. Allow them to soak for at least 4 hours or overnight. Drain and rinse before using.

Blend Ingredients:
- In a blender or food processor, combine the soaked macadamia nuts, nutritional yeast, lemon juice, apple cider vinegar, minced garlic, fresh basil leaves, extra virgin olive oil, salt, and pepper.

Blend Until Smooth:
- Blend the ingredients until you achieve a smooth and creamy consistency. If the mixture is too thick, add water, one tablespoon at a time, until you reach the desired texture.

Adjust Seasoning:
- Taste the macadamia cheese and adjust the salt, pepper, or lemon juice to your liking.

Chill (Optional):
- For a firmer texture and to allow the flavors to meld, you can refrigerate the macadamia cheese for at least an hour before serving.

Serve:
- Use basil and lemon macadamia cheese as a spread on crackers, bread, or in sandwiches. It can also be a delightful addition to pasta or salad dishes.

Garnish (Optional):
- Garnish with additional fresh basil leaves or a drizzle of olive oil for extra flavor and presentation.

This basil and lemon macadamia cheese provides a unique and refreshing flavor profile, perfect for adding a touch of brightness to your plant-based dishes. Enjoy experimenting with different herbs and spices to customize the spread to your liking.

Vegan Brie

Ingredients:

- 1 cup raw cashews, soaked in water for at least 4 hours or overnight
- 2 tablespoons refined coconut oil, melted
- 1 tablespoon tapioca starch
- 2 tablespoons nutritional yeast
- 2 tablespoons lemon juice
- 1 clove garlic, minced
- 1/2 teaspoon salt
- 1/4 cup unsweetened plant-based yogurt (for fermentation)
- Vegan Brie mold or a small bowl lined with cheesecloth

Instructions:

Soak Cashews:
- Place the raw cashews in a bowl and cover them with water. Allow them to soak for at least 4 hours or overnight. Drain and rinse before using.

Blend Ingredients:
- In a blender, combine the soaked cashews, melted coconut oil, tapioca starch, nutritional yeast, lemon juice, minced garlic, and salt. Blend until smooth and creamy.

Ferment the Mixture:
- Transfer the mixture to a bowl and stir in the plant-based yogurt. Cover the bowl with a clean cloth and let it sit at room temperature for 24-48 hours to ferment. This step adds complexity and tanginess to the flavor.

Shape the Brie:
- Once the mixture has fermented, transfer it to a Brie mold or a small bowl lined with cheesecloth. Smooth the top with a spatula.

Chill:
- Refrigerate the shaped vegan Brie for at least 6 hours or overnight to allow it to set.

Serve:
- Carefully remove the Brie from the mold and serve it with crackers, bread, or fresh fruit.

Garnish (Optional):

- Optionally, you can garnish the vegan Brie with herbs, edible flowers, or a drizzle of olive oil for presentation.

This vegan Brie recipe provides a rich and creamy alternative to traditional dairy-based Brie. Enjoy the smooth texture and tangy flavor of this plant-based cheese in various dishes or as part of a vegan cheese platter.

Vegan Gouda

Ingredients:

- 1 cup raw cashews, soaked in water for at least 4 hours or overnight
- 1 cup unsweetened plant-based milk (e.g., soy, almond, or oat milk)
- 1/4 cup nutritional yeast
- 2 tablespoons tapioca starch
- 2 tablespoons refined coconut oil, melted
- 1 tablespoon apple cider vinegar
- 1 teaspoon miso paste
- 1 teaspoon smoked paprika
- 1 teaspoon onion powder
- 1 teaspoon garlic powder
- 1/2 teaspoon mustard powder
- 1/2 teaspoon salt (adjust to taste)
- Vegan Gouda mold or a small bowl lined with cheesecloth

Instructions:

Soak Cashews:
- Place the raw cashews in a bowl and cover them with water. Allow them to soak for at least 4 hours or overnight. Drain and rinse before using.

Blend Ingredients:
- In a blender, combine the soaked cashews, plant-based milk, nutritional yeast, tapioca starch, melted coconut oil, apple cider vinegar, miso paste, smoked paprika, onion powder, garlic powder, mustard powder, and salt. Blend until smooth and creamy.

Heat the Mixture:
- Transfer the blended mixture to a saucepan over medium heat. Stir continuously until the mixture thickens and becomes stretchy. This usually takes about 5-7 minutes.

Shape the Gouda:
- Once the mixture has thickened, transfer it to a Gouda mold or a small bowl lined with cheesecloth. Smooth the top with a spatula.

Chill:
- Refrigerate the shaped vegan Gouda for at least 6 hours or overnight to allow it to set.

Serve:

- Carefully remove the Gouda from the mold and serve it sliced or grated.

Garnish (Optional):
- Optionally, you can garnish the vegan Gouda with smoked paprika, herbs, or a drizzle of olive oil for presentation.

This vegan Gouda recipe provides a creamy and flavorful alternative to traditional dairy-based Gouda. Enjoy it on sandwiches, crackers, or as part of a vegan cheese platter.

Spicy Sriracha Cheese

Ingredients:

- 1 cup raw cashews, soaked in water for at least 4 hours or overnight
- 1/4 cup nutritional yeast
- 2 tablespoons Sriracha sauce (adjust to taste)
- 2 tablespoons lemon juice
- 2 tablespoons refined coconut oil, melted
- 1 tablespoon tapioca starch
- 1 teaspoon garlic powder
- 1/2 teaspoon onion powder
- 1/2 teaspoon smoked paprika
- 1/2 teaspoon salt (adjust to taste)
- Water (as needed for blending)

Instructions:

Soak Cashews:
- Place the raw cashews in a bowl and cover them with water. Allow them to soak for at least 4 hours or overnight. Drain and rinse before using.

Blend Ingredients:
- In a blender, combine the soaked cashews, nutritional yeast, Sriracha sauce, lemon juice, melted coconut oil, tapioca starch, garlic powder, onion powder, smoked paprika, and salt. Blend until smooth and creamy.

Adjust Seasoning:
- Taste the mixture and adjust the Sriracha sauce or salt to your liking. Add more Sriracha for extra heat.

Heat the Mixture (Optional):
- If you want a stretchier texture like melted cheese, transfer the blended mixture to a saucepan over medium heat. Stir continuously until the mixture thickens and becomes stretchy. This usually takes about 5-7 minutes.

Chill (Optional):
- Refrigerate the spicy Sriracha cheese for at least 2-4 hours to allow it to set. This step is optional if you prefer a firmer texture.

Serve:
- Use the spicy Sriracha cheese as a spread on crackers, bread, or as a dip. It's also great for melting on nachos or in spicy grilled cheese sandwiches.

Garnish (Optional):
- Optionally, you can garnish the spicy Sriracha cheese with additional smoked paprika or chopped fresh herbs for presentation.

Enjoy the bold and spicy flavors of this homemade Sriracha cheese in your favorite dishes! Adjust the level of spiciness according to your preference.

Walnut and Cranberry Cheese Ball

Ingredients:

- 1 cup raw cashews, soaked in water for at least 4 hours or overnight
- 1/2 cup dried cranberries, chopped
- 1/2 cup walnuts, finely chopped
- 2 tablespoons nutritional yeast
- 1 tablespoon lemon juice
- 1 clove garlic, minced
- 1/2 teaspoon onion powder
- Salt and pepper to taste
- Fresh herbs (e.g., parsley or chives) for coating (optional)

Instructions:

Soak Cashews:
- Place the raw cashews in a bowl and cover them with water. Allow them to soak for at least 4 hours or overnight. Drain and rinse before using.

Blend Ingredients:
- In a food processor, combine the soaked cashews, chopped dried cranberries, nutritional yeast, lemon juice, minced garlic, onion powder, salt, and pepper. Blend until you achieve a smooth and creamy consistency.

Shape into a Ball:
- Transfer the mixture to a bowl and mix in half of the finely chopped walnuts. Shape the mixture into a ball.

Coat with Walnuts:
- Roll the cheese ball in the remaining finely chopped walnuts, ensuring an even coating.

Chill:
- Refrigerate the Walnut and Cranberry Cheese Ball for at least 1-2 hours to allow it to firm up and for the flavors to meld.

Serve:
- Place the cheese ball on a serving platter and surround it with crackers, sliced baguette, or vegetable sticks.

Garnish (Optional):
- Optionally, garnish the cheese ball with fresh herbs like parsley or chives for added color and flavor.

Enjoy this Walnut and Cranberry Cheese Ball as a festive and flavorful addition to your appetizer spread. It's perfect for gatherings or as a delicious snack.

Vegan Parmesan

Ingredients:

- 1 cup raw cashews
- 3 tablespoons nutritional yeast
- 1 teaspoon garlic powder
- 1/2 teaspoon onion powder
- 1/2 teaspoon salt

Instructions:

Prepare Cashews:
- If you haven't done so already, roast the raw cashews in a dry pan over medium heat until they are lightly golden. Allow them to cool.

Blend Ingredients:
- In a food processor or blender, combine the roasted cashews, nutritional yeast, garlic powder, onion powder, and salt.

Pulse until Crumbly:
- Pulse the ingredients until you achieve a crumbly texture. Be careful not to over-blend, or it may turn into a paste.

Adjust Seasoning:
- Taste the vegan Parmesan and adjust the seasoning to your preference. You can add more nutritional yeast or salt if needed.

Store:
- Transfer the vegan Parmesan to a sealed container and store it in the refrigerator. It can be kept for several weeks.

Usage:

- Sprinkle vegan Parmesan over pasta, salads, soups, roasted vegetables, or any dish where you would typically use Parmesan cheese.

This homemade vegan Parmesan provides a cheesy and savory flavor without any dairy. It's a versatile condiment that adds a delightful touch to various dishes. Feel free to experiment with the proportions to match your taste preferences.

Vegan Queso Dip

Ingredients:

- 1 cup raw cashews, soaked in water for at least 4 hours or overnight
- 1 cup unsweetened plant-based milk (such as almond, soy, or oat milk)
- 1/4 cup nutritional yeast
- 1/4 cup pickled jalapeños, chopped
- 1/4 cup pickled jalapeño brine (liquid from the jar)
- 2 tablespoons tomato paste
- 1 tablespoon olive oil
- 1 teaspoon ground cumin
- 1 teaspoon chili powder
- 1/2 teaspoon garlic powder
- 1/2 teaspoon onion powder
- Salt to taste
- Fresh cilantro or green onions for garnish (optional)

Instructions:

Soak Cashews:
- Place the raw cashews in a bowl and cover them with water. Allow them to soak for at least 4 hours or overnight. Drain and rinse before using.

Blend Ingredients:
- In a blender, combine the soaked cashews, plant-based milk, nutritional yeast, chopped pickled jalapeños, pickled jalapeño brine, tomato paste, olive oil, ground cumin, chili powder, garlic powder, and onion powder. Blend until smooth and creamy.

Adjust Consistency:
- If the queso is too thick, you can add more plant-based milk, a tablespoon at a time, until you achieve your desired consistency.

Adjust Seasoning:
- Taste the queso and adjust the salt and spices according to your preference. For more heat, you can add extra jalapeños or a pinch of cayenne pepper.

Warm on Stove (Optional):
- Transfer the queso to a saucepan and warm it over low-medium heat, stirring continuously until heated through. Be cautious not to overheat to maintain a creamy texture.

Serve:
- Pour the vegan queso dip into a bowl and garnish with fresh cilantro or green onions if desired.

Enjoy:
- Serve the queso with tortilla chips, nachos, tacos, or any other dish where you'd enjoy a cheesy dip.

This Vegan Queso Dip is not only delicious but also versatile and perfect for parties, gatherings, or as a tasty snack. Adjust the spice level and consistency to suit your taste.

Pine Nut Cheese Spread

Ingredients:

- 1 cup raw pine nuts
- 2 tablespoons nutritional yeast
- 2 tablespoons lemon juice
- 1 clove garlic, minced
- 1/4 cup water (adjust for desired consistency)
- 1/4 cup fresh basil leaves, packed
- Salt and pepper to taste

Instructions:

Soak Pine Nuts:
- Place the raw pine nuts in a bowl and cover them with water. Allow them to soak for at least 4 hours or overnight. Drain and rinse before using.

Blend Ingredients:
- In a blender or food processor, combine the soaked pine nuts, nutritional yeast, lemon juice, minced garlic, water, and fresh basil leaves. Blend until smooth and creamy.

Adjust Consistency:
- If the spread is too thick, you can add more water, one tablespoon at a time, until you reach your desired consistency.

Adjust Seasoning:
- Taste the pine nut cheese spread and add salt and pepper according to your preference. You can also adjust the lemon juice or nutritional yeast for added flavor.

Chill (Optional):
- For a firmer texture and to allow the flavors to meld, you can refrigerate the pine nut cheese spread for at least an hour before serving.

Serve:
- Transfer the spread to a bowl and serve it with crackers, bread, or vegetable sticks.

Garnish (Optional):
- Optionally, you can garnish the pine nut cheese spread with a drizzle of olive oil, pine nuts, or additional fresh basil leaves.

This pine nut cheese spread is a delicious and elegant option for a plant-based appetizer or snack. Enjoy the creamy texture and rich flavor on your favorite crackers or as a spread in sandwiches.

Truffle Almond Cheese

Ingredients:

- 1 cup raw almonds, soaked in water for at least 4 hours or overnight
- 2 tablespoons nutritional yeast
- 2 tablespoons lemon juice
- 1 clove garlic, minced
- 2 tablespoons white truffle oil
- 1/2 teaspoon white truffle salt (or regular salt, adjust to taste)
- Water (as needed for blending)
- Optional: Chopped fresh chives for garnish

Instructions:

Soak Almonds:
- Place the raw almonds in a bowl and cover them with water. Allow them to soak for at least 4 hours or overnight. Drain and rinse before using.

Blend Ingredients:
- In a food processor or high-speed blender, combine the soaked almonds, nutritional yeast, lemon juice, minced garlic, white truffle oil, and truffle salt. Blend until smooth and creamy, adding water as needed for the desired consistency.

Adjust Seasoning:
- Taste the truffle almond cheese and adjust the salt or truffle oil to your liking. The flavor should have a noticeable truffle essence.

Shape (Optional):
- If you want to shape the cheese, transfer the mixture to a piece of cheesecloth or a mold lined with plastic wrap. Twist and squeeze to shape it into a round or log.

Chill (Optional):
- For a firmer texture and enhanced flavors, refrigerate the truffle almond cheese for at least 2-4 hours.

Serve:
- Place the truffle almond cheese on a serving platter and garnish with chopped fresh chives if desired.

Enjoy:
- Serve the truffle almond cheese with crackers, crusty bread, or sliced vegetables. It's also a delightful addition to a vegan cheese board.

This truffle almond cheese is a sophisticated and delicious plant-based option, perfect for special occasions or when you want to indulge in a luxurious treat. Adjust the truffle oil and salt according to your taste preferences.

Pesto Cashew Cheese

Ingredients:

- 1 cup raw cashews, soaked in water for at least 4 hours or overnight
- 1 cup fresh basil leaves, packed
- 2 tablespoons nutritional yeast
- 2 tablespoons lemon juice
- 2 cloves garlic, minced
- 1/4 cup extra virgin olive oil
- Salt and pepper to taste
- Water (as needed for blending)
- Optional: Pine nuts for garnish

Instructions:

Soak Cashews:
- Place the raw cashews in a bowl and cover them with water. Allow them to soak for at least 4 hours or overnight. Drain and rinse before using.

Blend Ingredients:
- In a blender or food processor, combine the soaked cashews, fresh basil leaves, nutritional yeast, lemon juice, minced garlic, and extra virgin olive oil. Blend until smooth and creamy, adding water as needed for the desired consistency.

Adjust Seasoning:
- Taste the pesto cashew cheese and adjust the salt, pepper, or lemon juice to your liking.

Chill (Optional):
- For a firmer texture and to allow the flavors to meld, you can refrigerate the pesto cashew cheese for at least an hour before serving.

Serve:
- Transfer the pesto cashew cheese to a bowl and garnish with pine nuts if desired.

Enjoy:
- Serve the pesto cashew cheese as a spread on crackers, bread, or as a dip for vegetables. It's also a delicious addition to pasta dishes or as a topping for pizza.

This pesto cashew cheese is a delightful plant-based alternative that brings the vibrant flavors of pesto to your table. Experiment with the ratio of basil, garlic, and lemon juice to suit your taste preferences.

Chipotle Cashew Cheese

Ingredients:

- 1 cup raw cashews, soaked in water for at least 4 hours or overnight
- 2 chipotle peppers in adobo sauce (adjust to taste)
- 2 tablespoons nutritional yeast
- 2 tablespoons lemon juice
- 1 clove garlic, minced
- 2 tablespoons extra virgin olive oil
- 1/2 teaspoon smoked paprika
- 1/2 teaspoon ground cumin
- Salt to taste
- Water (as needed for blending)

Instructions:

Soak Cashews:
- Place the raw cashews in a bowl and cover them with water. Allow them to soak for at least 4 hours or overnight. Drain and rinse before using.

Prepare Chipotle Peppers:
- Remove the seeds from the chipotle peppers if you prefer a milder spice. Be cautious, as chipotle peppers can be quite hot.

Blend Ingredients:
- In a blender or food processor, combine the soaked cashews, chipotle peppers, nutritional yeast, lemon juice, minced garlic, extra virgin olive oil, smoked paprika, ground cumin, and salt. Blend until smooth and creamy, adding water as needed for the desired consistency.

Adjust Seasoning:
- Taste the chipotle cashew cheese and adjust the salt, chipotle peppers, or other seasonings to your liking.

Chill (Optional):
- For a firmer texture and to allow the flavors to meld, you can refrigerate the chipotle cashew cheese for at least an hour before serving.

Serve:
- Transfer the chipotle cashew cheese to a bowl and serve it as a spread on crackers, bread, or as a dip for vegetables.

Enjoy:

- Use the chipotle cashew cheese as a flavorful topping for tacos, nachos, or as a sandwich spread. Get creative with its versatile, smoky-spicy goodness.

This chipotle cashew cheese adds a bold and smoky kick to your plant-based dishes. Adjust the level of spiciness according to your taste preferences.

Vegan Nacho Cheese Sauce

Ingredients:

- 1 cup raw cashews, soaked in water for at least 4 hours or overnight
- 1 cup unsweetened plant-based milk (e.g., almond, soy, or oat milk)
- 1/4 cup nutritional yeast
- 1/4 cup pickled jalapeños, chopped (adjust to taste)
- 2 tablespoons pickled jalapeño brine (liquid from the jar)
- 2 tablespoons tomato paste
- 1 tablespoon arrowroot powder or cornstarch
- 1 tablespoon olive oil
- 1 teaspoon garlic powder
- 1 teaspoon onion powder
- 1 teaspoon ground cumin
- 1/2 teaspoon smoked paprika
- 1/2 teaspoon turmeric powder (for color)
- Salt to taste
- Optional: A pinch of cayenne pepper for extra heat

Instructions:

Soak Cashews:
- Place the raw cashews in a bowl and cover them with water. Allow them to soak for at least 4 hours or overnight. Drain and rinse before using.

Blend Ingredients:
- In a blender, combine the soaked cashews, plant-based milk, nutritional yeast, chopped pickled jalapeños, pickled jalapeño brine, tomato paste, arrowroot powder (or cornstarch), olive oil, garlic powder, onion powder, ground cumin, smoked paprika, turmeric powder, and salt. Blend until smooth.

Cook on Stove:
- Transfer the blended mixture to a saucepan and cook over medium heat, stirring continuously until the mixture thickens. This usually takes about 5-7 minutes.

Adjust Seasoning:
- Taste the nacho cheese sauce and adjust the salt or other seasonings to your liking. If you prefer more heat, add a pinch of cayenne pepper.

Serve:
- Pour the vegan nacho cheese sauce into a bowl and serve it warm with tortilla chips, nachos, or as a dip for vegetables.

Enjoy:
- This vegan nacho cheese sauce is perfect for movie nights, game days, or any occasion where you want a delicious and dairy-free cheesy treat.

Feel free to customize the recipe by adding other ingredients like diced tomatoes, green onions, or cilantro for added freshness and flavor.

Sun-Dried Tomato and Basil Cashew Cheese

Ingredients:

- 1 cup raw cashews, soaked in water for at least 4 hours or overnight
- 1/2 cup sun-dried tomatoes (not in oil), soaked in hot water for 20-30 minutes
- 1/4 cup nutritional yeast
- 2 tablespoons lemon juice
- 2 cloves garlic, minced
- 1/4 cup fresh basil leaves, packed
- 2 tablespoons extra virgin olive oil
- Salt and pepper to taste
- Water (as needed for blending)

Instructions:

Soak Cashews and Sun-Dried Tomatoes:
- Place the raw cashews in one bowl and cover them with water. Place the sun-dried tomatoes in another bowl and cover them with hot water. Allow both to soak for at least 4 hours or overnight.

Prepare Ingredients:
- Drain the soaked cashews and sun-dried tomatoes.

Blend Ingredients:
- In a blender or food processor, combine the soaked cashews, drained sun-dried tomatoes, nutritional yeast, lemon juice, minced garlic, fresh basil leaves, extra virgin olive oil, salt, and pepper. Blend until smooth and creamy, adding water as needed for the desired consistency.

Adjust Seasoning:
- Taste the cashew cheese and adjust the salt, pepper, or lemon juice to your liking.

Chill (Optional):
- For a firmer texture and to allow the flavors to meld, you can refrigerate the cashew cheese for at least an hour before serving.

Serve:
- Transfer the sun-dried tomato and basil cashew cheese to a bowl and serve it as a spread on crackers, bread, or as a dip for vegetables.

Enjoy:

- This versatile cashew cheese can be used in wraps, sandwiches, or pasta dishes. It's a great addition to a vegan cheese platter.

Feel free to experiment with additional herbs or spices to customize the flavor of your sun-dried tomato and basil cashew cheese. Enjoy the rich and savory taste of this plant-based spread!

Roasted Red Pepper and Walnut Spread

Ingredients:

- 1 cup walnuts, lightly toasted
- 2 large red bell peppers, roasted and peeled
- 2 cloves garlic, minced
- 2 tablespoons extra virgin olive oil
- 1 tablespoon tomato paste
- 1 tablespoon lemon juice
- 1 teaspoon smoked paprika
- Salt and pepper to taste
- Fresh parsley for garnish (optional)

Instructions:

Roast Red Peppers:
- Preheat the oven broiler. Place the red bell peppers on a baking sheet and broil, turning occasionally, until the skin is charred and blistered. Once roasted, place them in a bowl, cover with a kitchen towel, and let them steam for about 10 minutes. Peel off the skin, remove seeds, and chop the roasted peppers.

Toast Walnuts:
- In a dry skillet over medium heat, lightly toast the walnuts until fragrant. Be careful not to burn them.

Blend Ingredients:
- In a food processor, combine the toasted walnuts, chopped roasted red peppers, minced garlic, extra virgin olive oil, tomato paste, lemon juice, smoked paprika, salt, and pepper. Blend until you achieve a smooth and creamy consistency.

Adjust Seasoning:
- Taste the spread and adjust the salt, pepper, or lemon juice according to your preference.

Chill (Optional):
- For a firmer texture and to allow the flavors to meld, you can refrigerate the spread for at least an hour before serving.

Serve:
- Transfer the roasted red pepper and walnut spread to a bowl. Garnish with fresh parsley if desired.

Enjoy:
- Serve the spread as a dip for vegetables, a spread on crackers or bread, or as a flavorful addition to sandwiches and wraps.

This roasted red pepper and walnut spread is not only delicious but also provides a rich and nutty flavor with a hint of smokiness. It's a versatile condiment that can elevate a variety of dishes.

Vegan Blue Cheese

Ingredients:

- 1 cup raw cashews, soaked in water for at least 4 hours or overnight
- 1/4 cup unsweetened plain vegan yogurt
- 1 tablespoon nutritional yeast
- 1 tablespoon apple cider vinegar
- 1 teaspoon white miso paste
- 1 teaspoon lemon juice
- 1/2 teaspoon onion powder
- 1/2 teaspoon garlic powder
- 1/4 teaspoon salt
- 1/4 teaspoon spirulina powder (for color, optional)
- 1/4 cup vegan blue cheese mold (or a small bowl lined with cheesecloth)

Instructions:

Soak Cashews:
- Place the raw cashews in a bowl and cover them with water. Allow them to soak for at least 4 hours or overnight. Drain and rinse before using.

Blend Ingredients:
- In a blender or food processor, combine the soaked cashews, vegan yogurt, nutritional yeast, apple cider vinegar, white miso paste, lemon juice, onion powder, garlic powder, salt, and spirulina powder. Blend until smooth and creamy.

Transfer to Mold:
- Transfer the mixture to a vegan blue cheese mold or a small bowl lined with cheesecloth. Smooth the top with a spatula.

Set and Age (Optional):
- If you want a more authentic blue cheese flavor, you can allow the vegan blue cheese to set and age in the refrigerator for 24-48 hours.

Serve:
- Carefully remove the vegan blue cheese from the mold or cheesecloth and serve it on a cheese platter with crackers, bread, or fruit.

Garnish (Optional):
- Optionally, you can garnish the vegan blue cheese with additional herbs, crushed nuts, or edible flowers for presentation.

This vegan blue cheese provides a tangy and savory option for those looking to avoid dairy. Adjust the seasonings to your liking and experiment with the aging process for a more complex flavor.

Hemp and Chive Cream Cheese

Ingredients:

- 1 cup raw shelled hemp seeds (hemp hearts)
- 1/4 cup water
- 2 tablespoons nutritional yeast
- 2 tablespoons lemon juice
- 1 clove garlic, minced
- 2 tablespoons fresh chives, finely chopped
- Salt and pepper to taste

Instructions:

Blend Ingredients:
- In a food processor or blender, combine the raw hemp seeds, water, nutritional yeast, lemon juice, minced garlic, fresh chives, salt, and pepper.

Blend until Smooth:
- Blend the ingredients until you achieve a smooth and creamy consistency. If the mixture is too thick, you can add a bit more water to reach your desired texture.

Adjust Seasoning:
- Taste the hemp and chive cream cheese and adjust the salt, pepper, or lemon juice to your liking.

Chill (Optional):
- For a firmer texture and to allow the flavors to meld, you can refrigerate the cream cheese for at least 1-2 hours before serving.

Serve:
- Transfer the hemp and chive cream cheese to a bowl and serve it with bagels, crackers, or as a dip for vegetables.

Garnish (Optional):
- Optionally, you can garnish the cream cheese with additional fresh chives for a pop of color.

This hemp and chive cream cheese is not only tasty but also provides a good source of plant-based protein and healthy fats. Enjoy the creamy texture and herby flavor on your favorite snacks!

Cashew and Sundried Tomato Spread

Ingredients:

- 1 cup raw cashews, soaked in water for at least 4 hours or overnight
- 1/2 cup sun-dried tomatoes (not in oil), soaked in hot water for 20-30 minutes
- 2 cloves garlic, minced
- 2 tablespoons nutritional yeast
- 2 tablespoons lemon juice
- 2 tablespoons extra virgin olive oil
- 1/2 teaspoon dried oregano
- 1/2 teaspoon dried basil
- Salt and pepper to taste
- Water (as needed for blending)

Instructions:

Soak Cashews and Sun-Dried Tomatoes:
- Place the raw cashews in one bowl and cover them with water. Place the sun-dried tomatoes in another bowl and cover them with hot water. Allow both to soak for at least 4 hours or overnight.

Prepare Ingredients:
- Drain the soaked cashews and sun-dried tomatoes.

Blend Ingredients:
- In a food processor, combine the soaked cashews, drained sun-dried tomatoes, minced garlic, nutritional yeast, lemon juice, extra virgin olive oil, dried oregano, dried basil, salt, and pepper. Blend until smooth and creamy, adding water as needed for the desired consistency.

Adjust Seasoning:
- Taste the spread and adjust the salt, pepper, or other seasonings to your liking.

Serve:
- Transfer the cashew and sun-dried tomato spread to a bowl.

Enjoy:
- Use the spread on crackers, bread, or as a dip for vegetables. You can also toss it with pasta for a creamy and flavorful sauce.

This cashew and sun-dried tomato spread is a delicious and nutritious addition to your plant-based repertoire. Feel free to experiment with additional herbs or spices to suit your taste preferences.

Vegan Havarti

Ingredients:

- 1 cup raw cashews, soaked in water for at least 4 hours or overnight
- 1/4 cup refined coconut oil, melted
- 1/4 cup tapioca starch
- 1/4 cup nutritional yeast
- 2 tablespoons lemon juice
- 1 tablespoon white miso paste
- 1 teaspoon apple cider vinegar
- 1 teaspoon onion powder
- 1/2 teaspoon garlic powder
- 1/2 teaspoon salt (or to taste)
- 1/2 teaspoon lactic acid powder (optional, for added tanginess)
- 1/4 teaspoon white pepper (optional, for a milder flavor)

Instructions:

Soak Cashews:
- Place the raw cashews in a bowl and cover them with water. Allow them to soak for at least 4 hours or overnight. Drain and rinse before using.

Blend Ingredients:
- In a blender, combine the soaked cashews, melted coconut oil, tapioca starch, nutritional yeast, lemon juice, white miso paste, apple cider vinegar, onion powder, garlic powder, salt, lactic acid powder (if using), and white pepper (if using). Blend until smooth and creamy.

Heat Mixture:
- Transfer the blended mixture to a saucepan over medium heat. Stir continuously until the mixture thickens and becomes stretchy. This usually takes about 5-7 minutes.

Adjust Seasoning:
- Taste the Havarti mixture and adjust the salt or other seasonings according to your preference.

Mold the Cheese:
- Pour the Havarti mixture into a cheese mold or a small container lined with cheesecloth. Smooth the top with a spatula.

Chill:

- Refrigerate the Havarti for at least 4-6 hours or until it's firm and easy to slice.

Serve:
- Once chilled, remove the Havarti from the mold, and it's ready to be sliced and served.

Enjoy your homemade vegan Havarti on crackers, sandwiches, or cheese platters. This vegan version provides a similar creamy and mild experience to traditional Havarti. Adjust the seasonings and texture to suit your taste.

Vegan Swiss Cheese

Ingredients:

- 1 cup raw cashews, soaked in water for at least 4 hours or overnight
- 1/4 cup refined coconut oil, melted
- 1/4 cup tapioca starch
- 2 tablespoons nutritional yeast
- 1 tablespoon apple cider vinegar
- 1 tablespoon white miso paste
- 1 teaspoon Dijon mustard
- 1 teaspoon onion powder
- 1/2 teaspoon garlic powder
- 1/2 teaspoon salt (or to taste)
- 1/2 teaspoon lactic acid powder (optional, for added tanginess)
- 1/4 teaspoon white pepper (optional, for a milder flavor)

Instructions:

Soak Cashews:
- Place the raw cashews in a bowl and cover them with water. Allow them to soak for at least 4 hours or overnight. Drain and rinse before using.

Blend Ingredients:
- In a blender, combine the soaked cashews, melted coconut oil, tapioca starch, nutritional yeast, apple cider vinegar, white miso paste, Dijon mustard, onion powder, garlic powder, salt, lactic acid powder (if using), and white pepper (if using). Blend until smooth and creamy.

Heat Mixture:
- Transfer the blended mixture to a saucepan over medium heat. Stir continuously until the mixture thickens and becomes stretchy. This usually takes about 5-7 minutes.

Adjust Seasoning:
- Taste the Swiss cheese mixture and adjust the salt or other seasonings according to your preference.

Mold the Cheese:
- Pour the Swiss cheese mixture into a cheese mold or a small container lined with cheesecloth. Smooth the top with a spatula.

Chill:

- Refrigerate the Swiss cheese for at least 4-6 hours or until it's firm and easy to slice.

Serve:
- Once chilled, remove the Swiss cheese from the mold, and it's ready to be sliced and served.

Enjoy your homemade vegan Swiss cheese on sandwiches, in fondue, or wherever you would typically use Swiss cheese. Adjust the seasonings and texture to suit your taste.

Pistachio and Cranberry Cheese Log

Ingredients:

- 1 cup raw cashews, soaked in water for at least 4 hours or overnight
- 1/4 cup nutritional yeast
- 2 tablespoons lemon juice
- 1 clove garlic, minced
- 1/4 cup water
- Salt and pepper to taste
- 1/2 cup shelled pistachios, roughly chopped
- 1/2 cup dried cranberries, chopped
- Fresh herbs (such as parsley or chives) for garnish (optional)

Instructions:

Soak Cashews:
- Place the raw cashews in a bowl and cover them with water. Allow them to soak for at least 4 hours or overnight. Drain and rinse before using.

Blend Ingredients:
- In a food processor or blender, combine the soaked cashews, nutritional yeast, lemon juice, minced garlic, water, salt, and pepper. Blend until smooth and creamy.

Prepare Pistachios and Cranberries:
- Roughly chop the shelled pistachios and dried cranberries.

Mix In Pistachios and Cranberries:
- In a mixing bowl, combine the cashew mixture with the chopped pistachios and cranberries. Mix well until the ingredients are evenly distributed.

Shape into a Log:
- Lay out a piece of plastic wrap and transfer the cheese mixture onto it. Shape the mixture into a log, using the plastic wrap to help mold it. Roll the log in the plastic wrap and twist the ends to secure. Refrigerate for at least 2-3 hours or until firm.

Coat with Pistachios (Optional):
- If desired, you can roll the chilled log in additional chopped pistachios for an extra layer of crunch.

Garnish and Serve:

- Unwrap the log and place it on a serving platter. Garnish with fresh herbs if desired.

Enjoy:
- Serve the pistachio and cranberry cheese log with crackers, bread, or sliced vegetables. It makes a perfect appetizer for holiday gatherings or any festive occasion.

This vegan pistachio and cranberry cheese log is not only delicious but also adds a touch of elegance to your appetizer spread. Customize the flavor by adjusting the seasonings and enjoy the festive combination of textures and flavors.

Za'atar-Spiced Almond Cheese

Ingredients:

- 1 cup raw almonds, soaked in water for at least 4 hours or overnight
- 2 tablespoons nutritional yeast
- 2 tablespoons lemon juice
- 1 clove garlic, minced
- 1/4 cup water (adjust for consistency)
- 2 tablespoons za'atar spice blend
- Salt and pepper to taste
- Olive oil for garnish (optional)
- Sesame seeds for garnish (optional)

Instructions:

Soak Almonds:
- Place the raw almonds in a bowl and cover them with water. Allow them to soak for at least 4 hours or overnight. Drain and rinse before using.

Blend Ingredients:
- In a food processor or blender, combine the soaked almonds, nutritional yeast, lemon juice, minced garlic, water, za'atar spice blend, salt, and pepper. Blend until smooth and creamy, adding more water if needed for the desired consistency.

Adjust Seasoning:
- Taste the almond cheese and adjust the salt, pepper, or lemon juice to your liking. The za'atar spice blend is already flavorful, but you can add more if desired.

Shape (Optional):
- If you prefer, you can shape the almond cheese into a log or a round using plastic wrap or a mold.

Chill (Optional):
- For a firmer texture and to allow the flavors to meld, refrigerate the almond cheese for at least 1-2 hours.

Serve:
- Transfer the za'atar-spiced almond cheese to a serving dish. If desired, drizzle with olive oil and sprinkle sesame seeds on top.

Enjoy:

- Serve the almond cheese with crackers, bread, or as part of a mezze platter. The za'atar spice adds a Middle Eastern flair to this delightful vegan cheese.

Feel free to experiment with the amount of za'atar or incorporate other herbs and spices to suit your taste preferences. This vegan cheese is a great addition to your appetizer spread, especially for those who enjoy bold and unique flavors.

Vegan Beer Cheese

Ingredients:

- 1 cup raw cashews, soaked in water for at least 4 hours or overnight
- 1 cup vegan beer (choose a beer that complements your taste)
- 1/4 cup nutritional yeast
- 2 tablespoons arrowroot powder or cornstarch
- 2 tablespoons tomato paste
- 2 tablespoons soy sauce or tamari
- 1 tablespoon apple cider vinegar
- 1 teaspoon garlic powder
- 1 teaspoon onion powder
- 1/2 teaspoon smoked paprika
- 1/2 teaspoon mustard powder
- 1/4 teaspoon cayenne pepper (adjust to taste)
- Salt and black pepper to taste
- 2 tablespoons vegan butter or refined coconut oil
- 1 cup shredded vegan cheddar cheese

Instructions:

Soak Cashews:
- Place the raw cashews in a bowl and cover them with water. Allow them to soak for at least 4 hours or overnight. Drain and rinse before using.

Blend Ingredients:
- In a blender, combine the soaked cashews, vegan beer, nutritional yeast, arrowroot powder (or cornstarch), tomato paste, soy sauce, apple cider vinegar, garlic powder, onion powder, smoked paprika, mustard powder, cayenne pepper, salt, and black pepper. Blend until smooth.

Cook on Stove:
- Transfer the blended mixture to a saucepan over medium heat. Add vegan butter or refined coconut oil. Stir continuously until the mixture thickens.

Add Vegan Cheese:
- Once the mixture has thickened, reduce the heat to low and add the shredded vegan cheddar cheese. Stir until the cheese is fully melted and the mixture is smooth.

Adjust Seasoning:

- Taste the vegan beer cheese and adjust the salt, pepper, or other seasonings to your liking.

Serve:
- Pour the vegan beer cheese into a bowl or a bread bowl for serving.

Enjoy:
- Serve the vegan beer cheese with pretzels, bread, or vegetables for dipping. It's a perfect appetizer for game nights or gatherings.

This vegan beer cheese is rich, flavorful, and has the characteristic tanginess associated with traditional beer cheese. Adjust the spices and beer to suit your taste preferences.

Vegan Miso Butter

Ingredients:

- 1/2 cup vegan butter, softened
- 2 tablespoons white or light miso paste
- 1 tablespoon nutritional yeast
- 1 clove garlic, minced (optional)
- 1 teaspoon soy sauce or tamari
- 1 teaspoon maple syrup or agave nectar (optional)
- Black pepper, to taste
- Chopped fresh chives or green onions for garnish (optional)

Instructions:

Softening Vegan Butter:
- Allow vegan butter to soften at room temperature. This makes it easier to blend with other ingredients.

Mix Ingredients:
- In a bowl, combine the softened vegan butter, miso paste, nutritional yeast, minced garlic (if using), soy sauce, maple syrup (if using), and black pepper. Mix well until all ingredients are thoroughly combined.

Adjust Seasoning:
- Taste the miso butter and adjust the seasoning if necessary. You can add more miso for a stronger umami flavor, soy sauce for saltiness, or sweetener for balance.

Chill (Optional):
- For a firmer consistency and to allow the flavors to meld, you can refrigerate the miso butter for at least 30 minutes before serving.

Serve:
- Transfer the miso butter to a small bowl.

Garnish (Optional):
- Garnish with chopped fresh chives or green onions for an extra burst of flavor.

Enjoy:
- Use vegan miso butter as a spread on bread, crackers, or corn on the cob. It can also be melted and used as a savory topping for steamed vegetables, baked potatoes, or grilled tofu.

This vegan miso butter is a delightful combination of rich umami flavor and creamy texture. Feel free to adjust the ingredients to suit your taste preferences and experiment with different applications in your favorite dishes.

Turmeric and Black Pepper Cashew Cheese

Ingredients:

- 1 cup raw cashews, soaked in water for at least 4 hours or overnight
- 1/4 cup nutritional yeast
- 2 tablespoons lemon juice
- 1 clove garlic, minced
- 1 teaspoon turmeric powder
- 1/2 teaspoon black pepper, freshly ground
- 1/2 teaspoon onion powder
- 1/2 teaspoon salt (or to taste)
- Water (as needed for blending)

Instructions:

Soak Cashews:
- Place the raw cashews in a bowl and cover them with water. Allow them to soak for at least 4 hours or overnight. Drain and rinse before using.

Blend Ingredients:
- In a blender or food processor, combine the soaked cashews, nutritional yeast, lemon juice, minced garlic, turmeric powder, black pepper, onion powder, and salt. Blend until smooth and creamy, adding water as needed for the desired consistency.

Adjust Seasoning:
- Taste the cashew cheese and adjust the salt, black pepper, or lemon juice to your liking.

Chill (Optional):
- For a firmer texture and to allow the flavors to meld, you can refrigerate the cashew cheese for at least an hour before serving.

Serve:
- Transfer the turmeric and black pepper cashew cheese to a bowl.

Enjoy:
- Use it as a spread on crackers, bread, or as a dip for vegetables. You can also incorporate it into wraps, sandwiches, or pasta dishes for an extra burst of flavor and color.

This turmeric and black pepper cashew cheese not only provides a beautiful golden hue but also adds a warm and earthy flavor to your dishes. Experiment with the amount of turmeric and black pepper to suit your taste preferences.

Raspberry and Walnut Cream Cheese

Ingredients:

- 1 cup raw cashews, soaked in water for at least 4 hours or overnight
- 1/2 cup fresh raspberries
- 1/4 cup walnuts, chopped
- 2 tablespoons lemon juice
- 1 tablespoon nutritional yeast
- 1 clove garlic, minced (optional)
- 1/4 teaspoon salt (or to taste)
- Water (as needed for blending)

Instructions:

Soak Cashews:
- Place the raw cashews in a bowl and cover them with water. Allow them to soak for at least 4 hours or overnight. Drain and rinse before using.

Blend Ingredients:
- In a blender or food processor, combine the soaked cashews, fresh raspberries, chopped walnuts, lemon juice, nutritional yeast, minced garlic (if using), and salt. Blend until smooth and creamy, adding water as needed for the desired consistency.

Adjust Seasoning:
- Taste the cream cheese and adjust the salt or lemon juice to your liking.

Chill (Optional):
- For a firmer texture and to allow the flavors to meld, you can refrigerate the cream cheese for at least an hour before serving.

Serve:
- Transfer the raspberry and walnut cream cheese to a bowl.

Enjoy:
- Use it as a spread on bagels, toast, or crackers. This cream cheese also works well as a dip for fresh fruit or vegetables.

The combination of sweet raspberries and crunchy walnuts creates a unique and delightful flavor profile for this vegan cream cheese. Feel free to customize the recipe by adjusting the sweetness, adding more nuts, or incorporating other flavors to suit your taste.

Caramelized Onion and Thyme Almond Cheese

Ingredients:

For the Almond Cheese Base:

- 1 cup raw almonds, soaked in water for at least 4 hours or overnight
- 1/4 cup nutritional yeast
- 2 tablespoons lemon juice
- 1 clove garlic, minced
- 1/2 teaspoon salt
- Water (as needed for blending)

For the Caramelized Onion and Thyme Topping:

- 1 large onion, thinly sliced
- 2 tablespoons olive oil
- 1 teaspoon coconut sugar or brown sugar
- 1 teaspoon fresh thyme leaves
- Salt and pepper to taste

Instructions:

Almond Cheese Base:

Soak Almonds:
- Place the raw almonds in a bowl and cover them with water. Allow them to soak for at least 4 hours or overnight. Drain and rinse before using.

Blend Ingredients:
- In a blender or food processor, combine the soaked almonds, nutritional yeast, lemon juice, minced garlic, and salt. Blend until smooth and creamy, adding water as needed for the desired consistency.

Adjust Seasoning:
- Taste the almond cheese and adjust the salt or lemon juice to your liking.

Spread in a Dish:
- Transfer the almond cheese mixture to a dish, smoothing the top with a spatula. Set aside.

Caramelized Onion and Thyme Topping:

- Caramelize Onions:
    - In a skillet, heat olive oil over medium heat. Add the thinly sliced onions and cook, stirring occasionally, until they become golden brown and caramelized. This may take about 15-20 minutes.
- Add Sugar and Thyme:
    - Sprinkle coconut sugar (or brown sugar) over the caramelized onions and add fresh thyme leaves. Continue cooking for an additional 2-3 minutes, allowing the sugar to caramelize and the thyme to infuse its flavor. Season with salt and pepper to taste.
- Top Almond Cheese:
    - Spoon the caramelized onion and thyme mixture over the almond cheese in the dish, spreading it evenly.
- Chill (Optional):
    - For a firmer texture and to allow the flavors to meld, you can refrigerate the almond cheese with the topping for at least an hour before serving.
- Serve:
    - Serve the caramelized onion and thyme almond cheese with crackers, bread, or sliced vegetables.

This savory almond cheese with caramelized onions and thyme is a perfect addition to a cheese platter or appetizer spread. Adjust the seasoning and toppings according to your taste preferences.

Vegan Quesadilla Cheese

Ingredients:

- 1 cup raw cashews, soaked in water for at least 4 hours or overnight
- 1/4 cup nutritional yeast
- 2 tablespoons tapioca starch
- 1 tablespoon lemon juice
- 1 teaspoon apple cider vinegar
- 1/2 teaspoon garlic powder
- 1/2 teaspoon onion powder
- 1/2 teaspoon smoked paprika
- 1/2 teaspoon cumin powder
- 1/2 teaspoon salt (or to taste)
- 1/4 teaspoon turmeric powder (for color)
- 1 cup water
- 1 tablespoon agar-agar flakes or powder (optional, for firmness)

Instructions:

Soak Cashews:
- Place the raw cashews in a bowl and cover them with water. Allow them to soak for at least 4 hours or overnight. Drain and rinse before using.

Blend Ingredients:
- In a blender, combine the soaked cashews, nutritional yeast, tapioca starch, lemon juice, apple cider vinegar, garlic powder, onion powder, smoked paprika, cumin powder, salt, turmeric powder, and water. Blend until smooth.

Cook on Stove:
- Pour the mixture into a saucepan and cook over medium heat. Stir continuously to prevent lumps and ensure a smooth consistency. If you're using agar-agar for firmer texture, add it at this stage.

Thicken the Cheese:
- Continue cooking until the mixture thickens and becomes gooey and stretchy. This usually takes about 5-7 minutes.

Adjust Seasoning:
- Taste the vegan quesadilla cheese and adjust the salt or other seasonings to your preference.

Use or Cool and Slice:
- You can use the cheese immediately for your quesadillas or transfer it to a mold (if you want it to be sliceable) and let it cool in the refrigerator.

Slice and Melt:
- Once the cheese has cooled and solidified, slice it and use it as needed. When making quesadillas, the cheese will melt when heated.

Enjoy:
- Make your vegan quesadilla by placing the sliced cheese between tortillas and cooking until the cheese is melted and the tortillas are crispy.

Feel free to customize the seasonings to match your taste preferences, and enjoy your dairy-free quesadilla with this flavorful vegan cheese!

Vegan Greek-style Feta

Ingredients:

- 1 cup raw cashews, soaked in water for at least 4 hours or overnight
- 2 tablespoons lemon juice
- 2 tablespoons apple cider vinegar
- 3 tablespoons nutritional yeast
- 1 clove garlic, minced
- 1/2 cup extra virgin olive oil
- 1/4 cup water
- 1 teaspoon salt
- 1 teaspoon dried oregano
- 1/2 teaspoon dried basil
- 1/2 teaspoon dried thyme
- 1/4 teaspoon onion powder
- 1/4 teaspoon garlic powder

Instructions:

Soak Cashews:
- Place the raw cashews in a bowl and cover them with water. Allow them to soak for at least 4 hours or overnight. Drain and rinse before using.

Blend Ingredients:
- In a blender or food processor, combine the soaked cashews, lemon juice, apple cider vinegar, nutritional yeast, minced garlic, extra virgin olive oil, water, salt, dried oregano, dried basil, dried thyme, onion powder, and garlic powder. Blend until smooth and creamy.

Taste and Adjust:
- Taste the mixture and adjust the salt or other seasonings according to your preference.

Mold the Cheese:
- Transfer the mixture to a container or mold lined with cheesecloth. Press the mixture down to eliminate air bubbles.

Chill:
- Refrigerate the vegan feta for at least 4-6 hours or overnight to allow it to set and develop flavors.

Serve:

- Once chilled and set, you can remove the vegan feta from the mold. Cut it into cubes or crumble it, similar to traditional feta.

Enjoy:
- Use your vegan Greek-style feta in salads, wraps, pastries, or any dish where you would typically use feta cheese.

This vegan feta provides a creamy and tangy alternative with the characteristic flavors of Greek-style feta. Adjust the herbs and spices to your liking and experiment with different variations.

Vegan White Chocolate Cream Cheese

Ingredients:

- 1 cup raw cashews, soaked in water for at least 4 hours or overnight
- 1/4 cup coconut oil, melted
- 1/4 cup maple syrup or agave nectar
- 2 tablespoons lemon juice
- 1 teaspoon vanilla extract
- 1/4 cup cocoa butter, melted (for white chocolate flavor)
- 1/4 cup powdered sugar (adjust to taste)
- A pinch of salt

Instructions:

Soak Cashews:
- Place the raw cashews in a bowl and cover them with water. Allow them to soak for at least 4 hours or overnight. Drain and rinse before using.

Blend Ingredients:
- In a blender or food processor, combine the soaked cashews, melted coconut oil, maple syrup, lemon juice, vanilla extract, melted cocoa butter, powdered sugar, and a pinch of salt. Blend until smooth and creamy.

Adjust Sweetness:
- Taste the mixture and adjust the sweetness by adding more powdered sugar if needed.

Chill (Optional):
- For a firmer texture and to allow the flavors to meld, you can refrigerate the white chocolate cream cheese for at least 1-2 hours before serving.

Serve:
- Transfer the vegan white chocolate cream cheese to a bowl.

Enjoy:
- Use it as a spread on bagels, toast, or muffins. You can also use it in dessert recipes or as a dip for fruit.

This vegan white chocolate cream cheese offers a sweet and indulgent alternative to traditional cream cheese. Feel free to customize the sweetness and adjust the ingredients to suit your taste preferences.

Pecan and Cranberry Cheese Ball

Ingredients:

For the Cheese Ball:

- 1 1/2 cups raw cashews, soaked in water for at least 4 hours or overnight
- 1/4 cup nutritional yeast
- 3 tablespoons lemon juice
- 2 tablespoons white miso paste
- 1 clove garlic, minced
- 1/2 teaspoon onion powder
- 1/2 teaspoon salt
- 1/2 cup dried cranberries, finely chopped

For Coating:

- 1 cup pecans, finely chopped
- Fresh herbs (such as parsley or chives), finely chopped (optional)

Instructions:

Soak Cashews:
- Place the raw cashews in a bowl and cover them with water. Allow them to soak for at least 4 hours or overnight. Drain and rinse before using.

Prepare Coating:
- In a separate bowl, combine the finely chopped pecans and, if desired, fresh herbs. Mix well.

Blend Cheese Ball Ingredients:
- In a food processor, combine the soaked cashews, nutritional yeast, lemon juice, white miso paste, minced garlic, onion powder, and salt. Blend until smooth and creamy.

Mix in Cranberries:
- Transfer the cashew mixture to a bowl and fold in the finely chopped dried cranberries.

Shape the Cheese Ball:
- Using your hands, shape the mixture into a ball.

Coat the Cheese Ball:
- Roll the cheese ball in the prepared pecan and herb mixture, ensuring an even coating.

Chill:
- Place the coated cheese ball in the refrigerator for at least 1-2 hours to firm up.

Serve:
- Once chilled, transfer the pecan and cranberry cheese ball to a serving platter.

Enjoy:
- Serve the cheese ball with crackers, bread, or vegetable sticks. It's a delicious and festive appetizer.

This vegan pecan and cranberry cheese ball combines creamy and savory flavors with a hint of sweetness. Feel free to customize the recipe by adjusting the seasonings and coatings according to your taste preferences.

Vegan Ricotta Stuffed Shells

Ingredients:

For the Vegan Ricotta:

- 2 cups firm tofu, crumbled
- 1/4 cup nutritional yeast
- 2 tablespoons lemon juice
- 1 tablespoon olive oil
- 1 clove garlic, minced
- 1 teaspoon dried basil
- 1 teaspoon dried oregano
- Salt and pepper to taste

For the Stuffed Shells:

- 1 box jumbo pasta shells
- 3 cups marinara sauce (store-bought or homemade)
- Fresh basil or parsley for garnish (optional)

Instructions:

Vegan Ricotta:

Prepare Tofu:
- Crumble the firm tofu into a bowl.

Mix Ingredients:
- Add nutritional yeast, lemon juice, olive oil, minced garlic, dried basil, dried oregano, salt, and pepper to the crumbled tofu. Mix well to combine.

Stuffed Shells:

Cook Shells:
- Cook the jumbo pasta shells according to the package instructions. Drain and let them cool.

Preheat Oven:

- Preheat your oven to 350°F (175°C).

Assemble Stuffed Shells:
- Spoon a generous amount of the vegan ricotta mixture into each cooked pasta shell.

Arrange in Baking Dish:
- Place the stuffed shells in a baking dish.

Cover with Marinara Sauce:
- Pour the marinara sauce over the stuffed shells, covering them evenly.

Bake:
- Cover the baking dish with aluminum foil and bake in the preheated oven for about 25-30 minutes or until the shells are heated through.

Garnish and Serve:
- Remove from the oven and garnish with fresh basil or parsley if desired. Serve warm.

Enjoy:
- Enjoy your vegan ricotta stuffed shells as a comforting and satisfying main course.

These vegan ricotta stuffed shells are a flavorful and cruelty-free alternative to the traditional recipe. Customize the filling or sauce to suit your taste preferences, and serve them alongside a salad or crusty bread for a complete meal.

Vegan Pimento Cheese

Ingredients:

- 1 cup raw cashews, soaked in water for at least 4 hours or overnight
- 1/2 cup roasted red peppers, drained and chopped
- 1/4 cup nutritional yeast
- 2 tablespoons lemon juice
- 1 tablespoon white miso paste
- 1 teaspoon onion powder
- 1/2 teaspoon garlic powder
- 1/2 teaspoon smoked paprika
- 1/4 teaspoon turmeric (for color)
- 1/4 teaspoon cayenne pepper (optional, for heat)
- Salt and pepper to taste
- 1/2 cup vegan mayonnaise
- 1 cup shredded vegan cheddar cheese

Instructions:

Soak Cashews:
- Place the raw cashews in a bowl and cover them with water. Allow them to soak for at least 4 hours or overnight. Drain and rinse before using.

Blend Ingredients:
- In a blender or food processor, combine the soaked cashews, roasted red peppers, nutritional yeast, lemon juice, white miso paste, onion powder, garlic powder, smoked paprika, turmeric, cayenne pepper (if using), salt, and pepper. Blend until smooth.

Combine with Vegan Cheese:
- In a mixing bowl, combine the blended mixture with vegan mayonnaise and shredded vegan cheddar cheese. Mix until well combined.

Adjust Seasoning:
- Taste the pimento cheese and adjust the seasoning if necessary. You can add more salt, pepper, or other spices to suit your taste.

Chill (Optional):
- For enhanced flavor and texture, you can refrigerate the vegan pimento cheese for at least 1-2 hours before serving.

Serve:

- Use the vegan pimento cheese as a spread on sandwiches, as a dip with crackers or vegetables, or as a topping for baked potatoes or burgers.

This vegan pimento cheese captures the creamy, tangy, and slightly spicy flavors of traditional pimento cheese without any dairy. Feel free to customize the recipe by adding chopped jalapeños for extra heat or adjusting the spices to match your preferences.

Cumin and Coriander Seed Cheese

Ingredients:

- 1 cup raw cashews, soaked in water for at least 4 hours or overnight
- 1/4 cup nutritional yeast
- 2 tablespoons lemon juice
- 1 clove garlic, minced
- 1/2 teaspoon ground cumin
- 1/2 teaspoon ground coriander
- 1/2 teaspoon onion powder
- 1/2 teaspoon salt
- Water (as needed for blending)

Instructions:

Soak Cashews:
- Place the raw cashews in a bowl and cover them with water. Allow them to soak for at least 4 hours or overnight. Drain and rinse before using.

Blend Ingredients:
- In a blender or food processor, combine the soaked cashews, nutritional yeast, lemon juice, minced garlic, ground cumin, ground coriander, onion powder, and salt. Blend until smooth and creamy, adding water as needed for the desired consistency.

Adjust Seasoning:
- Taste the cashew cheese and adjust the salt, lemon juice, or spices to your liking.

Chill (Optional):
- For a firmer texture and to allow the flavors to meld, you can refrigerate the cumin and coriander seed cheese for at least 1-2 hours before serving.

Serve:
- Transfer the cashew cheese to a bowl.

Enjoy:
- Use it as a spread on crackers, bread, or as a dip for vegetables. This cumin and coriander seed cheese can also be a flavorful addition to wraps, sandwiches, or salads.

Feel free to experiment with the amount of cumin and coriander to achieve your desired level of flavor. This vegan cheese provides a rich and aromatic option for those who enjoy the warm and earthy notes of cumin and coriander.

Vegan Tzatziki

Ingredients:

- 1 cup plain vegan yogurt (almond, soy, or coconut-based)
- 1/2 cucumber, finely diced or grated
- 2 cloves garlic, minced
- 1 tablespoon fresh dill, chopped
- 1 tablespoon fresh mint, chopped (optional)
- 1 tablespoon extra virgin olive oil
- 1 tablespoon lemon juice
- Salt and pepper to taste

Instructions:

Prepare the Cucumber:
- If you're using a large cucumber, peel it and remove the seeds. Finely dice or grate the cucumber.

Drain Excess Water:
- Place the diced or grated cucumber in a fine-mesh sieve or cheesecloth. Sprinkle a pinch of salt over it and let it sit for about 10-15 minutes to drain excess water. Squeeze out any additional moisture.

Mix Ingredients:
- In a bowl, combine the vegan yogurt, minced garlic, chopped dill, chopped mint (if using), olive oil, and lemon juice. Mix well.

Add Cucumber:
- Fold in the drained cucumber into the yogurt mixture. Make sure the cucumber is evenly distributed.

Season:
- Season the tzatziki with salt and pepper to taste. Adjust the lemon juice or garlic if needed.

Chill (Optional):
- For enhanced flavor, refrigerate the tzatziki for at least 1-2 hours before serving.

Serve:
- Transfer the vegan tzatziki to a serving bowl.

Enjoy:

- Serve the tzatziki with pita bread, falafel, grilled vegetables, or as a refreshing dip for your favorite snacks.

This vegan tzatziki is a light and refreshing dip with the classic flavors of traditional tzatziki. Adjust the ingredient quantities to suit your taste preferences, and enjoy it as a versatile condiment in various dishes.

Walnut and Herb Stuffed Mushrooms

Ingredients:

- 16-20 large button or cremini mushrooms, cleaned and stems removed
- 1 cup walnuts, finely chopped
- 1/2 cup fresh breadcrumbs
- 2 tablespoons nutritional yeast
- 2 cloves garlic, minced
- 2 tablespoons fresh parsley, finely chopped
- 1 tablespoon fresh thyme leaves (or 1 teaspoon dried thyme)
- 1 tablespoon fresh rosemary, finely chopped (or 1 teaspoon dried rosemary)
- 1 tablespoon olive oil
- Salt and pepper to taste
- Lemon wedges for serving (optional)

Instructions:

Preheat Oven:
- Preheat your oven to 375°F (190°C).

Prepare Mushrooms:
- Clean the mushrooms and remove the stems. Place the mushroom caps on a baking sheet, ready for stuffing.

Prepare Filling:
- In a mixing bowl, combine the finely chopped walnuts, breadcrumbs, nutritional yeast, minced garlic, fresh parsley, thyme, rosemary, olive oil, salt, and pepper. Mix well until all ingredients are evenly combined.

Stuff the Mushrooms:
- Take a spoonful of the walnut and herb mixture and press it firmly into each mushroom cap, forming a mound.

Bake:
- Place the stuffed mushrooms in the preheated oven and bake for approximately 15-20 minutes or until the mushrooms are tender and the filling is golden brown.

Serve:
- Remove the stuffed mushrooms from the oven and let them cool for a few minutes before serving.

Optional Garnish:

- Garnish with additional fresh herbs or serve with lemon wedges for a burst of freshness.

Enjoy:
- Serve these walnut and herb-stuffed mushrooms as a delicious appetizer for parties or as a savory snack.

These stuffed mushrooms offer a delightful combination of earthy mushrooms, crunchy walnuts, and aromatic herbs. Feel free to customize the herbs and adjust the seasoning to suit your taste preferences.

Vegan Cheesecake with Berry Compote

Ingredients:

For the Vegan Cheesecake:

Crust:

- 1 1/2 cups graham cracker crumbs (ensure they are vegan)
- 1/4 cup melted coconut oil or vegan butter
- 2 tablespoons maple syrup

Filling:

- 2 cups raw cashews, soaked in water for at least 4 hours or overnight
- 1/2 cup coconut cream
- 1/2 cup lemon juice
- 1/2 cup maple syrup or agave nectar
- 1/2 cup melted coconut oil
- 1 teaspoon vanilla extract
- A pinch of salt

For the Berry Compote:

- 2 cups mixed berries (strawberries, blueberries, raspberries)
- 1/4 cup maple syrup
- 1 tablespoon lemon juice
- 1 teaspoon cornstarch mixed with 1 tablespoon water (optional, for thickening)

Instructions:

For the Vegan Cheesecake:

    Prepare the Crust:

- In a bowl, combine graham cracker crumbs, melted coconut oil or vegan butter, and maple syrup. Press the mixture into the base of a lined springform pan. Place it in the refrigerator while preparing the filling.

Prepare the Filling:
- In a blender, combine soaked cashews, coconut cream, lemon juice, maple syrup, melted coconut oil, vanilla extract, and a pinch of salt. Blend until smooth and creamy.

Assemble:
- Pour the filling over the crust in the springform pan. Smooth the top with a spatula.

Set:
- Place the cheesecake in the freezer for at least 4-6 hours or until set. You can also leave it in the freezer overnight.

For the Berry Compote:

Prepare the Compote:
- In a saucepan, combine mixed berries, maple syrup, and lemon juice. Cook over medium heat until the berries release their juices and the mixture thickens slightly.

Optional Thickening:
- If you prefer a thicker compote, you can mix cornstarch with water and add it to the berry mixture. Stir well and cook for an additional 1-2 minutes until thickened.

Cool:
- Allow the berry compote to cool before topping the cheesecake.

Assembly:

Top with Berry Compote:
- Once the cheesecake is set, remove it from the freezer and let it thaw for a few minutes. Pour the berry compote over the cheesecake.

Slice and Serve:
- Carefully remove the springform pan. Slice the cheesecake into portions and serve.

Enjoy:
- Enjoy your vegan cheesecake with luscious berry compote!

This vegan cheesecake with berry compote is a delightful and decadent dessert that's sure to please both vegans and non-vegans alike. Adjust the sweetness and thickness of the compote according to your taste preferences.

Cashew and Chive Cheese Ball

Ingredients:

For the Cashew and Chive Cheese:

- 2 cups raw cashews, soaked in water for at least 4 hours or overnight
- 1/4 cup nutritional yeast
- 1/4 cup fresh lemon juice
- 2 cloves garlic, minced
- 1 teaspoon onion powder
- 1/2 teaspoon salt (or to taste)
- 1/4 cup chopped fresh chives
- 2 tablespoons chopped fresh parsley (optional, for color)

For Coating:

- 1/4 cup finely chopped chives
- 1/4 cup finely chopped nuts (such as almonds or walnuts)

Instructions:

Soak Cashews:
- Place the raw cashews in a bowl and cover them with water. Allow them to soak for at least 4 hours or overnight. Drain and rinse before using.

Blend Cashew Cheese:
- In a food processor, combine the soaked cashews, nutritional yeast, fresh lemon juice, minced garlic, onion powder, and salt. Blend until smooth and creamy.

Add Chives and Parsley:
- Add the chopped chives and parsley (if using) to the cashew mixture. Pulse a few times to incorporate the herbs evenly into the cheese.

Shape into a Ball:
- Scoop the cashew mixture onto a piece of plastic wrap. Shape it into a ball, using the plastic wrap to help mold it. Place it in the refrigerator for at least 1-2 hours to firm up.

Prepare Coating:
- Combine the finely chopped chives and nuts on a plate or shallow dish.

Coat the Cheese Ball:

- Roll the chilled cashew cheese ball in the chive and nut mixture, ensuring an even coating.

Chill (Optional):
- For a firmer texture and to allow the flavors to meld, you can refrigerate the cheese ball for an additional 1-2 hours before serving.

Serve:
- Transfer the cashew and chive cheese ball to a serving platter.

Enjoy:
- Serve with crackers, bread, or vegetable sticks. It makes for a delicious and visually appealing appetizer.

Feel free to adjust the herbs and seasonings to suit your taste preferences. This vegan cashew and chive cheese ball is a flavorful and crowd-pleasing option for gatherings and parties.

Vegan Pepper Jack Cheese

Ingredients:

- 1 cup raw cashews, soaked in water for at least 4 hours or overnight
- 1/4 cup nutritional yeast
- 2 tablespoons lemon juice
- 2 tablespoons apple cider vinegar
- 1/2 cup water
- 2 tablespoons tapioca starch
- 1 teaspoon onion powder
- 1 teaspoon garlic powder
- 1 teaspoon salt
- 1 teaspoon smoked paprika
- 1/2 teaspoon ground cayenne pepper (adjust to taste for spiciness)
- 1/2 teaspoon ground black pepper
- 1 jalapeño, seeded and finely chopped (optional, for extra heat)

Instructions:

Soak Cashews:
- Place the raw cashews in a bowl and cover them with water. Allow them to soak for at least 4 hours or overnight. Drain and rinse before using.

Blend Ingredients:
- In a blender, combine the soaked cashews, nutritional yeast, lemon juice, apple cider vinegar, water, tapioca starch, onion powder, garlic powder, salt, smoked paprika, cayenne pepper, and black pepper. Blend until smooth.

Cook on Stove:
- Pour the mixture into a saucepan and cook over medium heat. Stir continuously to prevent lumps and ensure a smooth consistency.

Thicken the Cheese:
- Continue cooking until the mixture thickens and becomes gooey and stretchy. This usually takes about 5-7 minutes.

Add Jalapeño (Optional):
- If you want extra heat, add the finely chopped jalapeño to the cheese mixture and stir well.

Adjust Seasoning:

- Taste the vegan Pepper Jack cheese and adjust the salt, spices, or lemon juice as needed.

Use or Cool and Slice:
- You can use the cheese immediately for recipes like quesadillas, or transfer it to a mold (if you want it to be sliceable) and let it cool in the refrigerator.

Slice and Melt:
- Once the cheese has cooled and solidified, slice it and use it as needed. When melting, it should achieve a creamy consistency.

Enjoy:
- Incorporate the vegan Pepper Jack cheese into your favorite dishes like quesadillas, sandwiches, or nachos.

Feel free to adjust the level of spiciness by modifying the amount of cayenne pepper and adding or omitting the jalapeño. This vegan Pepper Jack cheese provides a zesty and flavorful alternative to traditional dairy-based options.

Vegan Tandoori Cheese

Ingredients:

For the Cashew Cheese:

- 2 cups raw cashews, soaked in water for at least 4 hours or overnight
- 1/4 cup nutritional yeast
- 2 tablespoons lemon juice
- 1 clove garlic, minced
- 1 teaspoon ground cumin
- 1 teaspoon ground coriander
- 1 teaspoon smoked paprika
- 1/2 teaspoon ground turmeric
- 1/2 teaspoon garam masala
- 1/2 teaspoon salt
- 1/4 teaspoon cayenne pepper (adjust to taste for spiciness)
- Water (as needed for blending)

For the Tandoori Marinade:

- 2 tablespoons vegan yogurt
- 1 tablespoon tomato paste
- 1 tablespoon vegetable oil
- 1 teaspoon ground cumin
- 1 teaspoon ground coriander
- 1 teaspoon smoked paprika
- 1 teaspoon ground turmeric
- 1 teaspoon garam masala
- 1 teaspoon chili powder (adjust to taste for spiciness)
- Salt to taste

Instructions:

Cashew Cheese:

   Soak Cashews:
   - Place the raw cashews in a bowl and cover them with water. Allow them to soak for at least 4 hours or overnight. Drain and rinse before using.

   Blend Cashew Cheese:

- In a blender or food processor, combine the soaked cashews, nutritional yeast, lemon juice, minced garlic, ground cumin, ground coriander, smoked paprika, ground turmeric, garam masala, salt, and cayenne pepper. Blend until smooth, adding water as needed for the desired consistency.

Tandoori Marinade:

Prepare Marinade:
- In a bowl, mix together vegan yogurt, tomato paste, vegetable oil, ground cumin, ground coriander, smoked paprika, ground turmeric, garam masala, chili powder, and salt. Adjust the spices to your taste.

Combine with Cashew Cheese:
- Transfer the blended cashew cheese to a bowl, and fold in the Tandoori marinade until well combined.

Marinate:
- Cover the bowl and let the Tandoori cheese marinate in the refrigerator for at least 2-4 hours, allowing the flavors to meld.

Serve:
- Serve the vegan Tandoori cheese with crackers, flatbreads, or as part of a charcuterie board.

This vegan Tandoori cheese brings together the creamy texture of cashew cheese with the bold and aromatic flavors of Tandoori spices. Adjust the spice levels to suit your taste preferences and enjoy this unique and flavorful vegan cheese option.

Vegan Garlic and Herb Boursin

Ingredients:

- 1 1/2 cups raw cashews, soaked in water for at least 4 hours or overnight
- 3 tablespoons nutritional yeast
- 2 tablespoons lemon juice
- 2 cloves garlic, minced
- 1 teaspoon onion powder
- 1 teaspoon dried basil
- 1 teaspoon dried parsley
- 1/2 teaspoon dried thyme
- 1/2 teaspoon dried rosemary
- 1/2 teaspoon dried dill
- 1/2 teaspoon salt (or to taste)
- 1/4 teaspoon ground black pepper
- 2 tablespoons refined coconut oil, melted (for richness)
- 2 tablespoons fresh chives, finely chopped (for mixing in)

Instructions:

Soak Cashews:
- Place the raw cashews in a bowl and cover them with water. Allow them to soak for at least 4 hours or overnight. Drain and rinse before using.

Blend Cashew Mixture:
- In a food processor or blender, combine the soaked cashews, nutritional yeast, lemon juice, minced garlic, onion powder, dried basil, dried parsley, dried thyme, dried rosemary, dried dill, salt, and black pepper. Blend until smooth and creamy.

Add Melted Coconut Oil:
- While the processor is running, gradually add the melted coconut oil to the cashew mixture. Blend until well incorporated.

Adjust Seasoning:
- Taste the mixture and adjust the salt or other seasonings to your liking.

Fold in Fresh Chives:
- Transfer the cashew mixture to a bowl and fold in the finely chopped fresh chives for an extra burst of flavor.

Chill (Optional):

- For a firmer texture and to allow the flavors to meld, you can refrigerate the garlic and herb Boursin for at least 1-2 hours before serving.

Serve:
- Transfer the vegan garlic and herb Boursin to a serving dish.

Enjoy:
- Serve with crackers, bread, or as a spread for sandwiches. This vegan cheese is a versatile and tasty addition to your plant-based culinary repertoire.

Feel free to customize the herb blend based on your preferences. This vegan garlic and herb Boursin provides a creamy, herby spread with a hint of garlic—perfect for entertaining or enjoying as a snack.

Vegan Cheesy Kale Chips

Ingredients:

- 1 bunch of kale, washed and thoroughly dried
- 2 tablespoons nutritional yeast
- 1 tablespoon olive oil
- 1 tablespoon lemon juice
- 1 teaspoon garlic powder
- 1/2 teaspoon onion powder
- 1/2 teaspoon smoked paprika
- Salt, to taste

Instructions:

Preheat Oven:
- Preheat your oven to 325°F (163°C).

Prepare Kale:
- Remove the stems from the kale leaves and tear the leaves into bite-sized pieces.

Massage Kale:
- In a large bowl, combine the kale pieces with olive oil, lemon juice, nutritional yeast, garlic powder, onion powder, smoked paprika, and a pinch of salt. Massage the kale with your hands, ensuring that the leaves are evenly coated with the seasoning mixture.

Arrange on Baking Sheets:
- Spread the seasoned kale leaves in a single layer on baking sheets. Avoid overcrowding to ensure they crisp up evenly.

Bake:
- Bake in the preheated oven for approximately 15-20 minutes or until the kale chips are crispy and slightly golden. Keep an eye on them to prevent burning.

Cool:
- Allow the kale chips to cool on the baking sheets for a few minutes. They will continue to crisp up as they cool.

Serve:
- Once cooled, transfer the kale chips to a serving bowl.

Enjoy:

- Enjoy your vegan cheesy kale chips as a healthy and flavorful snack.

Feel free to adjust the seasonings to suit your taste preferences. These vegan cheesy kale chips are not only delicious but also packed with nutrients, making them a fantastic alternative to store-bought chips.

www.ingramcontent.com/pod-product-compliance
Lightning Source LLC
LaVergne TN
LVHW081603060526
838201LV00054B/2051